MW01596855

Summary of

Triggers

by Marshall Goldsmith and Mark Reiter

Instaread

Please Note

This is a summary with analysis.

Copyright © 2016 by Instaread. All rights reserved worldwide. No part of this publication may be reproduced or transmitted in any form without the prior written consent of the publisher.

Limit of Liability/Disclaimer of Warranty: The publisher and author make no representations or warranties with respect to the accuracy or completeness of these contents and disclaim all warranties such as warranties of fitness for a particular purpose. The author or publisher is not liable for any damages whatsoever. The fact that an individual or organization is referred to in this document as a citation or source of information does not imply that the author or publisher endorses the information that the individual or organization provided. This concise summary is unofficial and is not authorized, approved, licensed, or endorsed by the original book's author or publisher.

Table of Contents

Overview

Triggers, written by executive coach Marshall Goldsmith, with Mark Reiter, his agent and writing partner, is a non-fiction self-help book designed for people who need motivation, understanding, and concrete, practical tools to effect lasting behavioral changes. Triggers are stimuli that prompt a behavioral reaction; they can be beliefs, behaviors, or environments. Identifying triggers is useful in all interpersonal relationships, whether in the workplace or at home. Being able to work consciously and proactively with triggers in one's ever-changing environment, and knowing how to identify and anticipate them, are key to career success, strengthened relationships, and becoming the best version of oneself.

There are two vital aspects of creating effective strategies to react constructively to triggers. A person has to have the desire to change and be ready to take responsibility for his or her actions no matter how challenging the external circumstances may be. Incorporating a daily practice of asking oneself engaging questions about one's effort to meet goals, as opposed to relying on external measures of progress, sets the foundation for accountability and long-term change. While behavioral transformation may not be easy, with the right attitude, support, and practices, it's entirely possible to bridge the gap between one's "real" self and one's "ideal" self.

Important People

Marshall Goldsmith is a world-renowned executive coach and bestselling author. Collectively, his books have sold more than two million copies and have been translated into 30 languages. He teaches executive education at Dartmouth College's Tuck School of Business.

Mark Reiter is a literary agent and writer who has collaborated with Goldsmith on two other books, *Mojo* (2010) and *What Got You Here Won't Get You There* (2007).

Key Takeaways

1. Behavioral change is often thwarted by triggering beliefs, such as "I have willpower and won't give in to temptation" and "My change will be permanent, and I will never have to worry again."

2. Various environments, such as a stressful work meeting or gridlocked highway, trigger different kinds of behavior.

3. A feedback loop can be very effective in behavior modification. The four stages of a feedback loop are evidence, relevance, consequence, and action.

4. Triggers can be productive or counterproductive, nudging someone toward behavior that either supports or thwarts his or her best self.

5. To analyze problematic behavior, it's necessary to break down the behavior into a sequence: trigger, which leads to impulse, which leads to awareness, which leads to choice, which leads to behavior.

6. At the start of the day, it's easy to have a plan, but harder to enact that plan as the day goes along. Having a strategy for keeping actions in alignment with plans is crucial to success.

7. When seeking behavioral change, there are four options for reacting to any given situation: creating, preserving, eliminating, and accepting.

8. Asking oneself a daily list of engaging questions can help monitor progress and maintain accountability to long-term objectives by increasing motivation, demonstrating commitment, focusing on positive action, and reinforcing the idea that goals are achieved incrementally.

9. When deciding whether or not to engage with a situation or trigger, it is helpful to ask, "Am I willing to make an effort to create a positive outcome in this situation?"

10. To prepare for optimal outcomes in challenging situations, ask four hourly questions focused on short-term gains and behavioral goals.

Thank you for purchasing this Instaread book

**Download the Instaread mobile app to get
unlimited text & audio summaries
of bestselling books.**

Visit Instaread.co
to learn more.

Analysis

Key Takeaway 1

Behavioral change is often thwarted by triggering beliefs, such as "I have willpower and won't give in to temptation" and "My change will be permanent, and I will never have to worry again."

Analysis

For most, lasting behavioral change can be very difficult to achieve, often due to lack of awareness or understanding about which behavior patterns need to change or how environment impacts behavior. It's human nature to resist change. People might feel overconfident in their willpower or think that their behavior is superior simply because others' behavior is objectively worse than their own. Or there could be an element of magical thinking that regards change not as a continuous road but as a sudden, finite destination. These beliefs can prevent people from trying to change and therefore lead to regret.

Denial, too, is often present in those who need to change, but resist taking action. For example, a man might eat or smoke too much, but be unwilling to admit that his behavior is problematic. A common tale among alcoholics is a drastic turn of alcohol-related events that prompts the type of introspection required for real change. But this change still doesn't happen overnight. Under the rubrics of self-help programs, change is viewed as something that is both desirable and attainable through a relatively quick process. In fact, it requires concerted attention and directed thoughts.

In *The Secret,* author Rhonda Byrne touts the power of positive thinking as a methodology of transforming oneself and, by extension, one's circumstances. [1] While her approach of asking, believing, and receiving may differ from Goldsmith's more practical methodology, both theories indicate that subconscious beliefs can leave people stuck in undesirable situations simply because they are not aware of the beliefs that hold them back. By becoming aware of such beliefs, the process of change can begin. Once a person has awareness, the difference between Goldsmith's and Byrne's respective ideas is stark: Goldsmith suggests concrete action, whereas Byrne is of the passive "ask, believe, receive" school of thought.

Key Takeaway 2

Various environments, such as a stressful work meeting or gridlocked highway, trigger different kinds of behavior.

Analysis

While it may not always be possible to control an uncomfortable exchange with a colleague or a curveball thrown in the midst of a high-pressure deadline, controlling the response and reaction to triggers is always possible. Paying attention to behavior in different situations leads to an understanding of how people are influenced by the current environment, positively or negatively.

For instance, if a man tends to spend too much money while hanging out with a certain extravagant friend, he first must realize the link between his bad habits and the environment in which these habits flourish. If a young woman knows that her mother incites frustrated, abrasive responses, she can take extra care to watch her reactions, especially if her reserves are depleted, either from physical or emotional stress. Though this is a common-sense approach to becoming one's best self, it's not always easy in the midst of a trigger.

Writer Amy Sutherland found a way to work with her environment at home when she found a solution to her marital discord by borrowing lessons from a book on training exotic animals. Instead of participating in a downward cycle of nagging, resentment, and explosive fights, she changed her own behavior in response to her husband's triggers by focusing on what he did well, as opposed to engaging with or even reacting to what bothered her. [2] Although she was eager to change his behavior, she wisely recognized that the best way to coexist in harmony might first be to change her own.

Key Takeaway 3

A feedback loop can be very effective in behavior modification. The four stages of a feedback loop are evidence, relevance, consequence, and action.

Analysis

Part of being able to enact lasting behavioral change is seeing a link between one's action and environment. For example, a young woman may learn that she is facing early-onset diabetes. This is the evidence stage of her feedback loop. In the relevance stage, she may then consider the diabetes behaviors that are in her control, such as her sugar-heavy diet. Believing that there is a link between her behavior and her health diagnosis, she understands the ramifications or consequences of her habits, and begins to take action to alter her health habits, including stress reduction. The healthier she becomes, the more she is spurred to act in ways that support her overall well-being.

Key Takeaway 4

Triggers can be productive or counterproductive, nudging someone toward behavior that either supports or thwarts his or her best self.

Analysis

Triggers are any type of stimuli that impact behavior. Under that broad umbrella, there are several different types of triggers: indirect and direct; external and internal; conscious and unconscious; encouraging or discouraging; and productive or counterproductive. Often, these categories overlap. For example, a woman might react negatively to her husband's behavior, possibly because she is upset about an upcoming anniversary of her father's death, and end up in a fight that results in a helpful visit to the couple's therapist that effectively strengthens their relationship.

Triggers indicate the role that environment plays in behavior. For example, a triggered response to a gossipy friend is to engage in gossip oneself in the attempt to garner attention or approval from that friend. But if the subject of this gossip realizes that a confidence was betrayed, that person may end the friendship. While this would not be something that the offending party consciously chose, it could still act as an instructive life lesson, one that is not easily forgotten and that could prompt a reflection on self-integrity that ultimately results in greater self-mastery.

Key Takeaway 5

To analyze problematic behavior, it's necessary to break down the behavior into a sequence: trigger, which leads to impulse, which leads to awareness, which leads to choice, which leads to behavior.

Analysis

What's more important than any particular trigger is a person's reaction to it. Therefore, thinking critically about the chain of events that follows from a trigger can also raise awareness and ultimately modify behavior. For example, if a man feels frequently manipulated by a co-worker into taking on more work, he can recognize that offering his help is not the best reaction to this particular trigger. When the co-worker asks for help because he is overwhelmed, he can first acknowledge his urge to pitch in. However, if his awareness has already been raised, he is more likely to think twice about putting aside his work and picking up the slack for his co-worker. He then realizes that he has a choice: he does not need to respond blindly to this request. It is in his power to say, "No, I'm sorry, but I can't do that right now," instead of suffering regret and resentment for having taken on something that was not his responsibility in the first place.

Key Takeaway 6

At the start of the day, it's easy to have a plan, but harder to enact that plan as the day goes along. Having a strategy for keeping actions in alignment with plans is crucial to success.

Analysis

Many times, the divide between what one plans to do and what one actually does is due to a miscalculation of personal energy levels that become depleted by the day's events, whether those are foreseen or unforeseen. Bridging this divide between planning and doing requires planning, for instance, by scheduling important meetings earlier in the day, when the energies are still available for the day's tasks and are aligned with motivation.

Experts agree that morning habits, like working out, are more likely to stick, because, when performed early in the day, these habits have a higher likelihood of becoming part of routine and not getting canceled due to waning energy levels. [3] In *The Artist's Way,* author Julia Cameron advocates a practice of morning pages, that is, writing nonstop for three pages. This is a way to ingrain better creative habits and problem-solving abilities that can last throughout the day and cultivate a lifelong creative practice. In her view, morning pages are effective because the tendency is to let ego-driven impulses and excuses get in the way first thing in the morning. [4] Doing something that is positive and constructive first thing in the morning can set a tone of accomplishment for the rest of the day.

Lessening the gap between planned accomplishments and actual accomplishments also builds confidence in the ability to effect behavioral change.

Key Takeaway 7

When seeking behavioral change, there are four options for reacting to any given situation: creating, preserving, eliminating, and accepting.

Analysis

Simply outlining the options for responding to triggers can be useful. With creating, for example, the action should, in some way, contribute to building or strengthening the sense of self. When faced with the prospect of chemo treatments, a cancer patient may decide to transform her time at the hospital from a depressing routine into a creative writing project, an essay on her experiences in which she taps her innate creativity and sense of humor to effectively cope with the situation.

A response of preserving maintains a valuable or positive aspect of the situation. For example, a graphic designer may be frustrated with a client's attitude, while also recognizing that the relationship is worth maintaining. She may combine creating with preserving, instituting a new policy or practice that lessens her stress around the situation, while keeping the relationship intact, such as allowing herself 24 hours to respond to any email.

Elimination means choosing to get rid of a practice or behavior that is standing in the way of long-term goals. For example, a cosmetic dermatologist may have a loyal cadre of patients, but the time she spends with them gets in the way of launching her own skin-care line. So, she may enact a plan to stop accepting new patients.

An accepting response is characterized by embracing a realistic assessment of a situation. Consider the scenario of the rapidly changing publishing industry. With physical bookstores becoming nearly extinct over the past several years, booksellers had two options: cling to the old way of doing business or seek out new and innovative opportunities. By accepting the changing face of the industry, the Harvard Book Store in Cambridge scored double-digit sales growth after installing in-store printing press that spoke to the consumer's growing need for instant gratification. [5] In this case, an accepting response led to a subsequent creative response.

Key Takeaway 8

Asking oneself a daily list of engaging questions can help monitor progress and maintain accountability to long-term objectives by increasing motivation, demonstrating commitment, focusing on positive action, and reinforcing the idea that goals are achieved incrementally.

Analysis

An engaging question is worded to incite a feeling of personal responsibility and demonstrate effort. One example of such a question would be, "Did I do my best to set clear goals?"

Asking oneself a specific set of engaging questions each night demonstrates a dedication to behavioral change. It also provides a mechanism for receiving feedback about current practices. The key to the daily questions' effectiveness is having another person, such as a friend or coach, respond to the answers and challenge any trouble spots, to determine if there is causal link between behaviors and an environmental factor.

Beyond job performance or career achievement, self-inquiry has the potential to heighten one's sense of well-being. In the yogic tradition, self-inquiry is useful because it directs practitioners back to themselves and helps them discover their true nature. [6]

Daily questions might uncover uncomfortable emotional truths. For example, if a man has trouble with money management, a daily set of questions that address spending could lead him to realize that he spends more frequently when he is confronting feelings of failure. Realizing this, he could experience emotional distress, as a sentiment of general unworthiness rises to his consciousness. However, this could ultimately be a healing and transformative moment when he realizes that his belief in his unworthiness is just that—a belief. Thus, taking honest stock of oneself and of personal behaviors can be empowering.

Social psychologists have observed that 40 percent of the time people aren't giving a lot of thought to what they are doing, so creating new habits always requires repetition and then that the behavior becomes ingrained in one's neural pathways. [7] In this context, the benefit of daily questioning is twofold: this practice both increases self-awareness and encourages behavioral change.

Key Takeaway 9

When deciding whether or not to engage with a situation or trigger, it is helpful to ask, "Am I willing to make an effort to create a positive outcome in this situation?"

Analysis

Pausing to gauge whether or not to engage with a triggering event can help determine the right action. This helps cultivate a Zen-like mindset, and reinforces the idea that the person performing the triggering behavior is coming from his or her own mindset and circumstances that likely have nothing to do with anyone else.

By not reacting, one can have freedom from feeling controlled by or at the mercy of external situations. Therefore, taking time to decide whether or not to engage can potentially free up energy. An employee might be fed up with her supervisor's requests to give up her personal time to do excessive team-building exercises. When her supervisor asks for what seems like the hundredth time if she can sacrifice a Saturday, she might pause to assess the situation before committing. If she doesn't do this, she might potentially respond in a hostile or obviously resentful manner, further deteriorating her relationship with her boss. The pause might help her view the request from a detached situation: perhaps she realizes that the supervisor isn't trying to make her life miserable, but is lonely because she focuses on work to the detriment of her personal life, and simply wants company. The woman's compassion for her boss can enable her to offer a more sincere and considerate response, even if she decides to politely decline the offer. This wisdom is summed up in a line from *Pooh's Instruction Book,* philosophical wisdom inspired by *Winnie-the-Pooh* author A.A. Milne: "Don't underestimate the value of Doing Nothing, of just going along, listening to all the things you can't hear, and not bothering." [8] This sentiment speaks to the importance of non-reaction and reminds us that we can choose to not let someone else's actions adversely affect us.

Key Takeaway 10

To prepare for optimal outcomes in challenging situations, ask four hourly questions focused on short-term gains and behavioral goals.

Analysis

Asking four questions ahead of time can help set powerful intentions and demonstrate commitment to being one's best self. The four questions measure effort, not outcome, and gauge whether or not people have done their best to create their own happiness and meaning.

The roots of this proactive methodology can be traced back to the positive psychology movement, founded by psychologist Martin Seligman, who has spent years researching the psychological benefits of focusing on what is positive, as opposed to what is negative. [9] Seligman's pioneering contributions paved the way for Goldsmith's proactive approach to behavioral change by introducing the idea that we have a degree of control over our psychological well-being and can choose to focus on the positive. Through this lens, the hourly questions are a way to raise self-awareness about the ability to meet challenges effectively and create an atmosphere of engagement and personal responsibility. They also lessen any tendency to adopt a mindset of victimhood, blaming, or the belief that one's own satisfaction and performance is in the hands of an external source.

Author's Style

Goldsmith uses anecdotes from his career as an executive coach, as well as from his personal life. He shares stories from friends, colleagues, and clients to illustrate principles in action. The cumulative effect of these stories is the impression that everyone, no matter their strengths or weaknesses, can benefit from behavioral change. Goldsmith is an academic and makes use of studies and theory about behavioral change, which bolster his argument's credibility. He lays out the information in a clear, concise way, explaining how certain methodologies, such as the daily questions practice, can be applied to any situation, personal or professional.

Author's Perspective

Goldsmith has been a leading executive coach and public speaker for more than 35 years. Based on his track record, he has full confidence that his techniques and approach to behavioral change work as long as people make a meaningful effort to change. Throughout his career, he has helped scores of highly successful people become more effective leaders and agents of change in their own lives. His lessons apply to anyone who needs motivation, support, and structure to change behavior and reactionary patterns. His perspective is that most people are in need of support, whether they find a coach, like him, or learn how to become their own coach, which is his ultimate goal.

~~~~ END OF INSTAREAD ~~~~

Thank you for purchasing this Instaread book

**Download the Instaread mobile app to get
unlimited text & audio summaries
of bestselling books.**

Visit Instaread.co
to learn more.

References

1. Byrne, Rhonda. *The Secret.* New York: Atria Books/Beyond Words, 2006, p.9.

2. Sutherland, Amy. "What Shamu Taught Me About a Happy Marriage." *New York Times.* June 25, 2006. Accessed March 9, 2016. http://www.nytimes.com/2006/06/25/fashion/25love.html?ex=1169438400&en=3edcee0d-461222fa&ei=5087&excamp=mkt_shamu

3. Newman, Hannah. "The complete guide to working out before work." *Quartz.* July 10, 2014. Accessed March 9, 2016. http://qz.com/221964/the-complete-guide-to-working-out-before-work/

4. Burkeman, Oliver. "This column will change your life: Morning Pages." *The Guardian.* October 3, 2014. Accessed March 9, 2016. http://www.theguardian.com/lifeandstyle/2014/oct/03/morning-pages-change-your-life-oliver-burkeman

5. Johnson, Phil. "The Man Who Took on Amazon and Saved a Bookstore." *Forbes.* May 10, 2012. Accessed March 9, 2016. http://www.forbes.com/sites/philjohnson/2012/05/10/the-man-who-took-on-amazon-and-saved-a-bookstore/#97c9cb942040

6. Adyashanti. "The Art of Self-Inquiry: How heart-centered questions of spiritual inquiry

can lead you on the path of awakening." Yoga International Blog. January 27, 2014. Accessed March 9, 2016. https://yogainternational.com/article/view/the-art-of-self-inquiry

7. Neal, D.T., et al. "The Pull of the Past: When Do Habits Persist Despite Conflict With Motives?" *Personality and Social Psychology Bulletin* 37:11(2011): 1428-37. Accessed March 27, 2016. http://psp.sagepub.com/content/37/11/1428

8. Milne, A.A. *Pooh's Instruction Book.* New York: Dutton, 1995, p.75.

9. [9] Seligman, Martin. *Authentic Happiness: Using the New Positive Psychology to Realize Your Potential for Lasting Fulfillment.* New York: Atria Books, 2004, p.6.

CPSIA information can be obtained
at www.ICGtesting.com
Printed in the USA
LVHW081522260219
608801LV00013B/178/P